The Nativity

Illustrated by Julie Vivas

Voyager Books

Harcourt Brace & Company

San Diego   New York   London

Printed in Singapore

In the days of Herod the King, the Angel Gabriel was sent from God to the city of Nazareth. To a virgin espoused to a man whose name was Joseph, and the virgin's name was Mary.

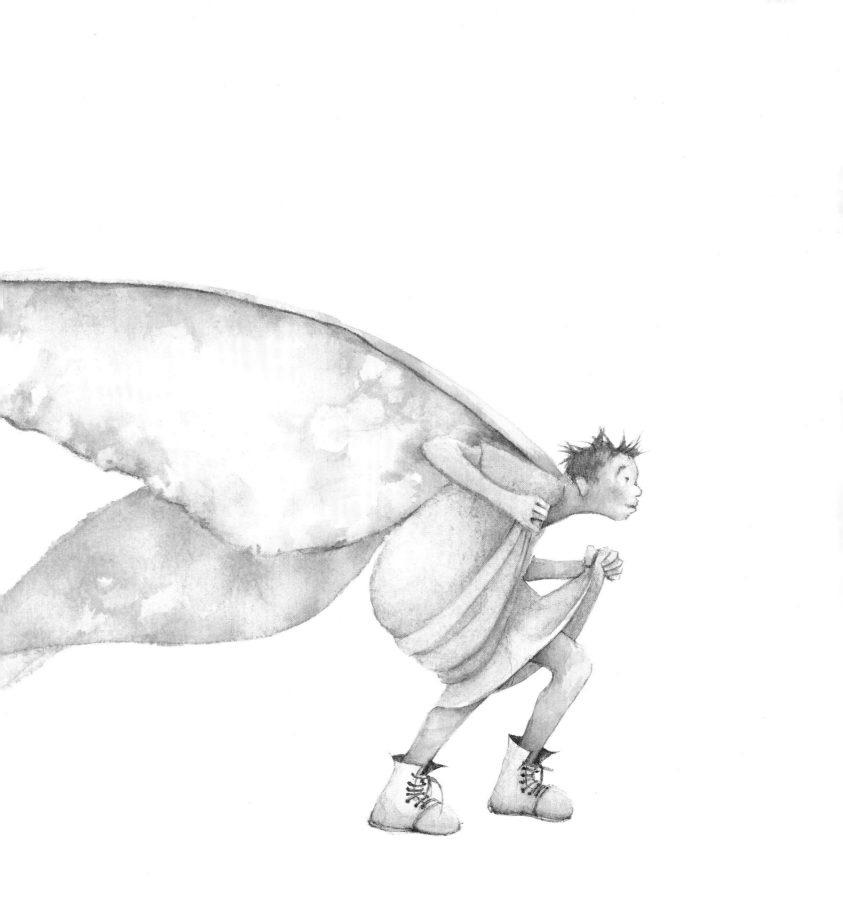

And the Angel said unto her "Hail! the Lord is with thee.
Blessed art thou among women."
And when she saw him she was troubled.

The Angel said, "Fear not Mary: for thou hast found favor with God. Thou shalt bring forth a son and call his name Jesus."

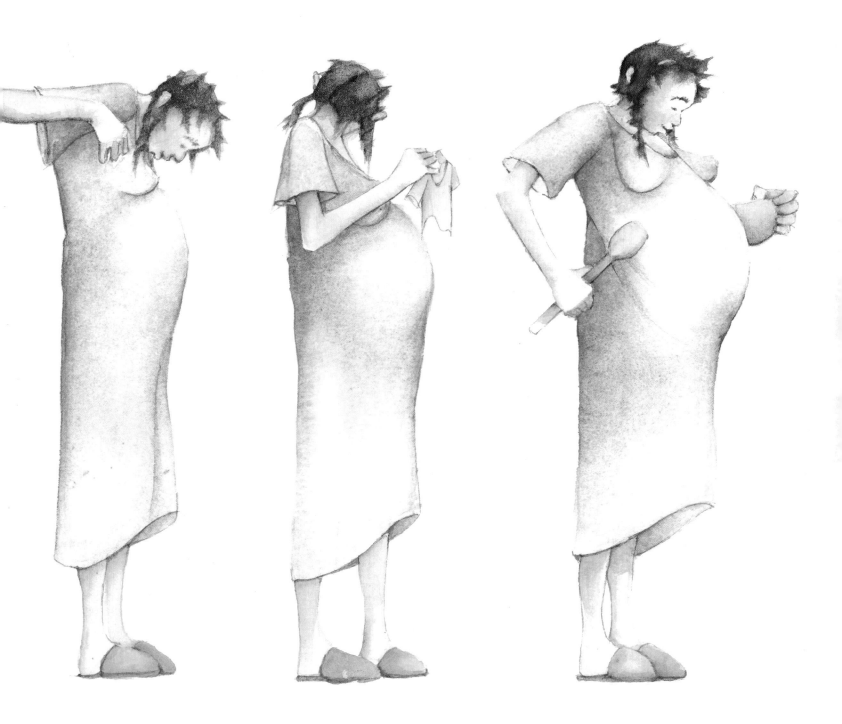

It came to pass that Caesar Augustus decreed that
all the world should be taxed, everyone to his own city.

So Joseph went from Nazareth to the city of Bethlehem, with Mary his wife being great with child.

And so it was that, while they were there, the day
came that she should be delivered.

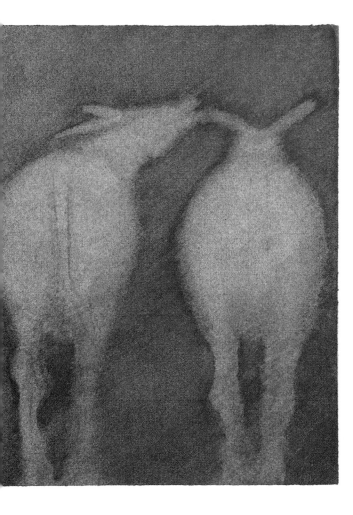

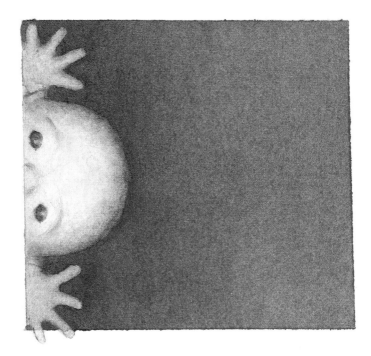

And she brought forth her firstborn son

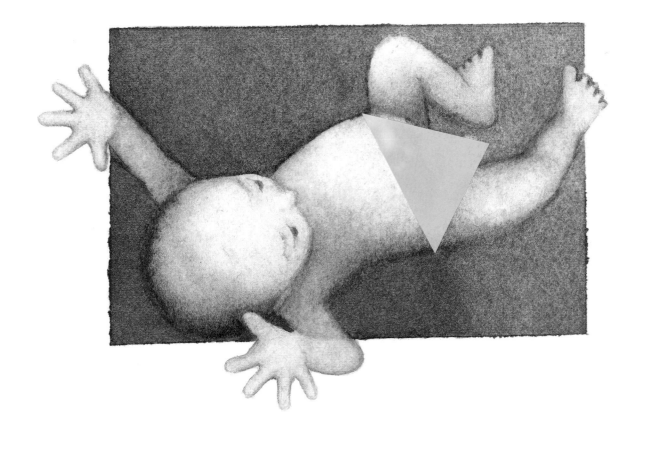

and wrapped him in swaddling clothes, and laid him in a manger, because there was no room for them in the inn.

There were in the same country shepherds in the field,
keeping watch over their flock by night.

When, lo, the Angel of the Lord came upon them and the glory
of the Lord shone around them and they were sore afraid.

And the Angel said, "Fear not, for I bring you
tidings of great joy. For unto you is born
this day in the city of David a Savior,
which is Christ the Lord.
And this shall be a sign; Ye shall find the babe
wrapped in swaddling clothes, lying in a manger."

And suddenly there was with the Angel a multitude of the heavenly
host praising God.

When the Angels were gone, the shepherds said to one another,
"Let us go into Bethlehem to see this thing which is come to pass."

And they came with haste, and found Mary, and Joseph, and the babe lying in a manger.

And behold, there came wise men to Jerusalem saying, "Where is He that is born King of the Jews? For we have seen His star and are come to worship Him."

And, lo, the star, which they saw in the East, went before them, till it stood over where the young child was.

When they were come into the house, they saw the young
child with Mary His mother, and fell down and
worshiped Him and when they had opened their treasures they
presented unto Him gifts of gold, and frankincense, and myrrh.

The wise men departed into their own country and the shepherds also returned, glorifying and praising God for all the things that they had heard and seen.

And the child was called Jesus, which was so named by the Angel, before He was conceived in the womb.

For Luis

First Published in Australia by Omnibus Books, Adelaide
First U.S. edition 1988

Voyager Books is a registered trademark of Harcourt Brace & Company.

Library of Congress Cataloging-in-Publication Data
The Nativity.
Text consists of excerpts from the authorized King James version of
the Bible.
"Voyager Books."
Summary: Illustrates the story of the birth of Jesus and the arrival of the
wise men and shepherds at the manger.
1. Jesus Christ—Nativity—Juvenile literature.
[1. Jesus Christ—Nativity. 2. Bible. N.T. Luke.]
1. Vivas, Julie, 1947– . ill.
BT315.A3 1988   232.9′2   87-23795
ISBN 0-15-200535-8
ISBN 0-15-200117-4 pb

J I

Printed in Singapore